NYX
Sister of Erebus

NYX
Sister of Erebus

A Memoir
of
My Mother's Alzheimer's

nancy genevieve

NOX Press

Nancy Genevieve (Perkins) gratefully acknowledges the support of the University of Illinois Springfield (UIS) for a 2009 Sabbatical to research and write this book: Board of Trustees, University of Illinois; UIS: Richard D. Ringeisen, Chancellor; Harry Berman, Provost and VCAA; Margot Duley, Dean of CLAS; Members of CSAC, Allan Cook, Chair; and Members of English Department, James Ottery, Chair; as well as the kind editors of the *Alchemist Review* who invited and published an earlier version of "Hold Back Tomorrow"(Spring 2010).

Nancy Genevieve is emerita associate professor of English at the University of Illinois Springfield. She is the author of *NYX: Mother of Light* (2001) and *NYX: Daughter of Chaos* (2002). Her writings have been shared at venues in KY, IL, NH, MI, and MA and have appeared in literary journals and other print media.

Printed:
The Eureka Printing Company
Eureka, Illinois

Cover Art:
Rhea Edge
May Discovery
Watercolor Intaglio Monoprint
2011

Author Photograph:
Author with her mother
James E. Kohl

To

Olivia, Jack

Samuel, Zachery, Kayla

George, Samuel

So you
may know
them.

Contents

Foreword

Nancy Genevieve's *NYX: Sister of Erebus* is the last book in the poet's trilogy inspired by NYX, the primal Greek goddess who was the personification of Night. *NYX: Mother of Light* was published in 2001, and *NYX: Daughter of Chaos* followed in 2002. Then, in 2004 Genevieve's poetry was celebrated in *Midwestern Miscellany* in an issue devoted to women poets of the Midwest. The article about her work was entitled "Fighting the Darkness: The Poetry of Nancy Genevieve." Since my friendship with Nancy Genevieve extends over 20 years now and I wrote the foreword for her second book, she has asked me to do the same for this last book. I am honored to do so because Nancy is one of the finest colleagues I have had in my entire career. We have worked together on several projects, shared ideas about writing and teaching, congratulated each other on our accomplishments, and cheered each other in those dark nights of the soul that sometimes occur in the academic world. As with her previous books, *NYX: Sister of Erebus* further explores life through the central metaphor of the darkness.

A good friend once said to me, "We humans are not capable of any maturity or real wisdom until we have experienced the sadness of the death of a parent." That may seem to be a bit extreme, but he then explained that to look down at a parent in the coffin makes us fully aware of the reality of death and, subsequently, of our own mortality. I have heard other people express almost the same idea: that maturity involves our coming to terms with the reality of death. It is as if we cannot live life to full measure unless we are aware of the darkness that awaits us. Such knowledge is essential in determining how we will live knowing that we will one day die. It should empower us to treat each other with kindness. One of life's consolations is that as we approach our own death we have memories which we have hoarded and cherished and even shared with others to make death seem not so terrible, especially if we have lived life fully. A real sadness is that some people may have those memories stolen from them by Alzheimer's as they face the darkness.

NYX: Sister of Erebus, Genevieve's third book of poems, is devoted to the loss of her parents, chiefly her mother, and to the cruelty of Alzheimer's, not so much to the mother herself, but to the husband and daughter who must cope with its gradual and relentless destruction of what once was a dynamic, loving woman. It is painful and sad enough when children have to become the parents of their own parents, and this truth is most harsh and almost unbearable when a parent is afflicted with Alzheimer's.

Consequently, the speaker in these poems has a focus that is somewhat bifurcated. Many of the poems are set in the present as she must deal with the painful reality of her mother's loss of memory, beginning with the first poem, "Hold Back Tomorrow," when the mother says, "I have a slight case of Alzheimer's." As the disease progresses, the speaker becomes a scribe who recalls memories of her parents and their shared experiences. It is as if the mother's inability to recall important experiences makes it imperative that the speaker recall these memories to celebrate the truth of long years of a truly loving marriage. "Hold Back Tomorrow" concludes with the mother, anticipating that she may become a burden to her husband and daughter, asking "What can I do to help?" But as the "thief" steals more and more memory from the mother, the question becomes the central concern and motivation for the speaker/daughter.

But these poems are not so much about the speaker/daughter but rather about the parents and their lives and, especially, about how their love was every bit as strong at the end as it was during World War II. The book is about parents and their fundamental strengths and enduring personalities. It is the story of complex emotions which undergird all loving human relationships.

One of the most important memories the speaker recalls is found in the powerful poem "Nightmares," the longest poem in the book. The speaker recalls that as a girl she was awakened by her father's nightmares of World War II and especially of her mother's comforting him against the darkness of those haunting memories. The mother's embrace assures him that "he is alive," that "the light will come in the morning," and that "the nazis did not win." This poem is especially important because it connects with the first poem when the mother, in trying to minimize the cruelty of Alzheimer's, says, "He's promised [...] he'll hold my hand all the way to the grave."

NYX: Sister of Erebus is an amazing reading experience. The speaker has written an extended work which captures great truth and wisdom about life. As such, it is a fitting third book in the poet's trilogy. As Genevieve has said to me, "Of course helping those we love to die with dignity is personally painful, but helping them to truly live with the fragments of themselves is much harder; it is very much like helping our children reach their independence and watching them struggle to do so—it's much easier to do the task—any task—for them."

Although the tone of this book is understandably sad because of the helplessness of people to provide much help to the loved one who finally does not even recognize them, it is a celebration of family love. Through the recollection of the past, the speaker conveys the love of husband and wife, of father and mother, of daughter and parents. The poems in the book fulfill the subtitle of "A Memoir of My Mother's Alzheimer's," but they also serve as a testimony to remind us that what is most important in facing the darkness is to live with kindness and to treat people, especially those close to us, with tenderness and love. Finally, the message that emerges in the varied poems in this book is that love is the answer. Whether it is addressed to a parent, friend, neighbor, or indeed to any human being, the book's central question "What can I do to help?" can be answered by four words: kindness, gentleness, gratitude, and love.

Loren Logsdon
Emeritus Professor of English
Eureka College (IL) and
Western Illinois University
Summer 2012

Preface

Two weeks after my daughter's wedding in 2001, I learned my mother had been diagnosed with Alzheimer's.

As a family we knew Mama had been listening to her own inner muse too much and making some day-to-day mistakes prior to the doctor's formal diagnosis. When I had hurried back to my familial home in 2000 to find out why Mama was in the hospital, she assured me from her hospital bed that she had "only an allergy reaction to some medicine." When I pushed for a more definitive answer, she said "the doctor said he'd write on my chart not to prescribe Viagra for me again."

Yes, we laughed; it was the only way not to cry all the time. Somehow she seemed to read emotions long after her words snarled their meaning. She would often laugh with us at some happy thought she no longer quite understood.

With this diagnosis, Mama and Daddy located a clinical study, and she volunteered to take the medicine or a placebo, "So maybe what we learn will someday help somebody else."

Mama lived in the home she and Daddy had built in 1957 until 2004 when Daddy believed he could no longer adequately care for her. He placed her in a locked Alzheimer's unit in a local nursing home. For the next two years, he drove across town every day in blizzard or in boiling heat to take her a Hershey bar, to tell her the latest news, and mostly, to tell her that he loved her. The final year of her life, when his own health declined, he moved too far away to see her every day, and the thread which connected them grew very thin, but it still held.

What I had envisioned for this book was the acceptance of the inevitable: growing, maturing, aging, dying . . . that is a part of this book. But. It is about so much more: it is about that which endures, that which is real, solid, strengthening not for the self, but for those we love. That is the final lesson my parents taught me: that sharing that love—the true-forever-and-always type, the type which helps us to be the best we can be, even in the locked ward of an Alzheimer's unit—is the one part of life to embrace throughout this whole wonderful journey.

This book is their story—their lesson. I am their scribe.

Acknowledgments

My writing, my living, occurs in the support and hearts of those who share tears and laughter, goodbyes and hellos. As I tuck in the corners and smooth the wrinkles from this book, I thank all of you who have cared so much.

This final book emerged from the comments of family, friends, colleagues, students, and strangers who heard me read from works-in-progress. To each and all of you who helped me live and write this work, a huge and loving THANK YOU!

Jim, who held my hand and guided my heart in all of my endeavors; Scott & Zaidy, Sarah & James, who lived through these events and helped me see through the darkness to the light—always; Loren, who has been a mentor, scholar, friend, and dreamer; Rhea, who shared her art and knowledge to create this cover which poignantly and beautifully captures the essence of these words; Sheila and Peg, who heard what I tried to write and then helped me to craft the words to say what I meant; Tom Daley, who taught, listened, cajoled, and encouraged my poetic voice; my poetry sisters at the Concord Poetry Workshop, who helped me draft after draft after draft with these poems and never let me get away with stopping too soon; Marilyn Walter, who cleaned up the frazzled ends of my typing and computing; Paul Burton, who heard what I wanted and translated it into print.

I also want to thank friends and family who cried and laughed and rolled up their sleeves and worked with me most of my life: Diane & Larry, Margo & Bob, Geneva & Howell, Judy & Mike, Kathy & Wayne, Gayle & John, Loren & Mary, Sheila, Peg & Mike, Jane, Bill & Carol, Ginny & Jerry, Lane, Barbara, Ethan, Dr. Pam & Tina, Barry & Annamae, Charlene & Joe, Sharon & Jim, Rev. Karen, Rev. John & Sarah Elizabeth, Rev. Tom & Carol, Rev. Rick . . . and Mama and Daddy.

ng
September 2012

Hold Back Tomorrow

Lazy ivory circles bleach the brown
as I pour cream into my morning coffee.

"The doctor said . . ."
        I watch swirls until they merge.
        She waits, studies my face
"I have a slight case of Alzheimer's."

A quick breath.
A newspaper rustle from across the room.

She props up her cheeks with a stiff smile
runs her fingers through her uncombed silver hair
tousled curls tumble to the collar of her teal housecoat.

"I took a test," she flutters, looks away
        straightens a single flow-blue plate
        on the wall just above the breakfast table.
"I . . . I took this test . . ."

One of those three identical plates
is missing, leaving a jagged hole
in the orderly line and a deeper blush of paint.

"The doctor said I nearly passed," she combs
        the fringe on her placemat with her fingernails.
"If only I had gotten just one more answer right
        I wouldn't have this disease."

Coffee burns my tongue
my hands sweep crumbs, refold napkins
align blue and white salt and pepper shakers.

"It could be worse. It could be worse.
I'll just fade away. Never feel pain."

       Mama sags back into her chair
"just . . . fade away."

Peering into the shallows of my cup, wanting
just wanting . . . what is already cooling
savoring . . .

"He's promised—"
       Daddy creases a page of his morning paper just so
       looks up, meets Mama's eyes, nods
"he'll hold my hand all the way to the grave."

—a catch in my breath—
I inhale   swallow
wipe my eyes with a folded napkin.

Mama's pale blue eyes skitter
       skim cobalt plates sauntering above cupboards
       dust the top of a ceramic duck's head
       holding a tea towel too pretty to use.

She leans forward
       her vein-roped hands   take my empty cup
       set it in a waiting saucer
       as her seamless voice flows
"What can I do to help?"

Constellations

> Night does not shatter
> and create stars.

black blackness of now
will glitter soon
with stories from before
books stilled them:

"Once there was . . ."
they will say
"but then there came . . ."
someone will continue
"and it was never ever . . ."

No one will add
even in a whisper
"they lived happily . . ."

The carved letters
bite away the stone. No one
reading it will notice
that it is the what-is-missing . . .

Night
      nearly
            filled the sky.

The moon
        a comma
            in the message.

Sunday

Every time they call, I have to talk to
        that woman-not-my-mother.

Her voice sounds like Mama's but spills
        words my mother would never say:
        "Then that slut in the restaurant
        dared to speak to me . . ."

Daddy's voice thickens as he stirs
        the bubbling meaning
        "Don't you remember Mary Katherine?
        We went to high school together?"

"No. Mary Katherine was young
        her hair golden.
        That painted hussy was old.
        Her chins sagged.
        She had roots showing.
        That woman, that woman . . ."

Her words
        flutter thrash float sink.

An interlude, a pause in a public prayer
        a cameo of
        the-woman-who-was . . .
        a memory brooch
        framed in lacy filigree
        straight-backed, church-proper . . .

"It's okay" leads Daddy
        "you liked your dumplin's
        and sweetened tea and
        all of your and my apple cobbler.
        You had a good lunch

didn't you? Wasn't the cornbread
particularly good today?"

This woman—
        a child led to a distracting toy—
        "That cook must've used
        crisco, none of those wimpy olive oil substitutes.
        Or maybe she used real lard.
        In a cast iron skillet. Yea, you can bet
        your ass. That was it."

Keep us

"We'll deal with that . . .
later" he says.
I don't push
when I move
from an hour away to five.

"We're fine
just minor aches and pains."
I pretend to believe
when Mama talks less
and Daddy more.

"Our routines keep us busy
I play golf and your mother
stays home and reads."
I try to be silent
when they won't answer.

"We like our home"
he looks away.
I let them go
because they will not stay.

Stained Glass

Mama fills four crystal decanters with water.
Drop-by-drop she adds whole bottles of food coloring
then lines them up on the sun-porch window ledges.

When the sun glides across the face of the house
rubies, emeralds, amethysts, and sapphires
shimmer auroras on the facing wall.

A pirouetting girlchild
bows to her silhouette on a stage of
fractured rainbows.

Descant

He

She walks right past me
      never slows her step
      just keeps on walking out the door.

I have to hurry
      she will not stop or look both ways—
      another lesson seeping out
      that slow leak into no more.

God forgive me
      for just a split second
      I wish her to keep walking.

She

I think I hear a lark
      beyond that blank blue wall.

I'll hurry or he'll fly away and
      I may never ever see
      a lark who calls my name.

The Layers

       wither
       tumble
       hide in the corner
wait
       for the chilling wind
       to blow them away.

Nightmares

"No. No! No!" careens thru this wall
of my once childhood bedroom   sleep-shattered awake
I breathe so very slowly   silently   round-eyed
not-listening   too frightened to forget   I am
forced to remember.

As sound asleep as his day senses will allow   Daddy
thrashes   fists flail night air   elbows   knees jab sheets
    feet kick the dark   one word   just one word
punches
the quiet   explodes   rounds   expands   takes form
    fills his room   my room   the whole house.

Infant faces rattle in oval frames   march down the
wall on mama's side of their bed   but for decades
    only his soft snores   soaked through this wall
filled all the corners . . .

I shudder   recognize the cry   of his war
    hear this battle echo   wait   for Mama
in a nanosecond of knowing that I'm a mother
    am barraged

    *what if she doesn't hear?   has forgotten the cause?   is paralyzed
in her own fear?   what if   oh god, what if   she can't   doesn't
remember anymore?   do I get up?   call to him?   cradle him to
awake?   dare I touch him?   tomorrow such recalled nightmares
    embarrass him . . . yet to ignore . . .*

I throw back the comforter   feel the cold floor
bite back the warmth   before I reach the doorknob
Mama's voice—*cool balm   night breath of mountain air*—
coaxes him   "Dear.   Dear.
You're having another nightmare.   You are here now.
You're at home.   You got out.   You're with me now.
It'll be okay.   It'll be okay."

Her hand on my forehead . . . iced my fevers   slowed the
licking tongues from burning   shut demon eyes from
searing   her fingers chilled measlesmumpschickenpox   lost
one-eyed doll   moved best friend   betrayed first love   all cooled
      all vanquished.

I was still pulling baby teeth   when I watched her grab a
foot-long butcher knife from the silverware drawer
search the whole house   even the basement   for the bad guy
she thought she had heard one night   while Daddy was
working the late shift   I couldn't image anyone stupid enough
to fight with her when she had that look burning the cobweb-
corners   but even she couldn't stop   Daddy's night demons
      they came by pretty regularly back then   she couldn't keep
them from coming back

One night   I just stood in the hallway   outside their
opened bedroom door   "Daddy was just having a nightmare"
she took my hand   led me back to bed   "nightmares can't hurt you
      they just live inside your head"   Well . . .   I didn't tell her
but anything just living inside my head   didn't sound like something
I wanted to catch   even from Daddy   so whenever Daddy started
shouting   I just pulled the covers   over my head   stuck my fingers
      in my ears   so those   things couldn't crawl inside my head
after they were finished with Daddy.

     I always knew his nightmare   came from World War II
and it wouldn't lie silently in that unmarked graveyard . . .
it lived in his head   slugged its way out   to his mind
     his mouth   his arms and legs.

Mama could make it hide   at least until dawn
     she had been doing that for at least fifty years.
but now   tomorrow?   next week? . . . next month?
     all the years to come?

who then?   who will soothe Daddy's forehead? interrupt
his terror?   when once again   in a night without stars
the nazis search the stalls in a German barn   for blankets
hoofed food   enemies   sleep   while Daddy and his buddies
lie more still than mice—in that loft with their top-secret-radio-
radar equipment   stashed beneath thin straw blankets of
camouflage—paralyzed in silence   which might   just might
keep them   alive?   knowing they could not   dared not
*   shift a cramped shoulder   peer between floor boards   load a*
chamber   pull a pin?   holding their collective breath   in dread
in hope of daylight?

Year by year   shard by shard   Daddy spoke phrases of
    that night   those nights   mostly he just held them
inside   sealed tight   war nights . . . maybe   just maybe
Mama knew   the whole   maybe not.

As close as I ever got to hearing that whole story   came
as Daddy turned over official documents stamped "Top
Secret" for me to give to my grown son   he had tucked
them away in some unknown place   saving them   hiding
them   from the enemy?   while handing them   to me
      without even opening the large envelope   he said
"These are so old now   I guess it is okay   that I give them
to you   just give them to him   I want him to know . . ."
      he stopped   turned away.

Every year a Christmas card arrived   with a name on the return
address I had never heard   it was stashed in the pile with all the others
*   "Daddy, who is this person?" I asked one Christmas as I began to*
prepare a mailing list for their Fiftieth Anniversary . . . "Just someone I
knew in the war" he mumbled and started to say no more.   That
Christmas   perhaps he was beginning to shed memories or share them
"That card is from his wife. I send her a card every year   to let her

know I still remember   He died over there   and I promised him
that I'd keep in touch with her . . . for him.   You know?"

Years later he recounted that German-barn-night
seated around my dining room table   so his oldest grandson
could record his story   but even then . . . he would stop . . .
edit the telling . . . before he continued . . .

More and more often   Mama leaves her side of the bed
in the still parts of the night   but says   over breakfast
"I had a good night's sleep   didn't you?"   but when I
     ask her about that water glass now in the kitchen sink—
which I had emptied   long before I turned out the lights
at midnight   after the nightly news   after they had said
their good nights   brushed their teeth   crawled into bed—
. . . she decides   to take a bite out of her sweet roll
unable to answer   because her mouth is full   Daddy just
glances at me   counts her sleeping pills   records the
morning number . . .

As her primary skills dilute   fade   and fade   and   fade
     there will be a night . . .
who then will remind Daddy   that he is   alive?
     who can make him   believe that the light
will come in the morning?   who will tell him   again
and again and again   that the nazis did not win
that night?   or this night?

When his silences rupture   flood the house with memories
too fierce to be calmed   when Mama is not near
enough to hear   her hands   have forgotten how to cool
     her words   have frozen in her mind   her covenant of
"for worse" silenced   I have returned to my life   a
thousand miles from this childhood bedroom . . .
     what then   what then?

Night sun

hung
on the lip of the horizon.

Thistled wind

poked holes

in October.

Once she was diagnosed

she began to hurry to do all that she had wanted to do all
along   private oil painting lessons   not the group ones
she could afford and had always taken   but private ones
which would get the work done . . . fast   well   as fast as
oil dries   she turned out another Turnerish blue ocean
one   gave it to me   because she said I loved the first
one so much   I had it framed with money made from
teaching an extra course   because that made her happy
too   a bouquet of quickly painted pink and white dog
wood blossoms interspersed with over-blown peonies
some in colors   like the purple one   I've never seen
living   but matching the lilac pitcher with its cobalt
handle on deep-ocean intense teals and turquoises
strokes with the abandoned freedom of a child swinging
with her head back racing the clouds   a new style for her
not the tiny brushed perfection of copying an Audubon
bird   another of a still life with black lines   outlining
reminiscent of a master whose work she had shown me as
a child in the Chicago Art Institute   a final one   mostly
blues and pinks streaks with yellow shooting smudges
racing   toward   toward   on the back wooden frame
she wrote *Dying Star*   and my name   she also wrote
the wrong year on it   those details are what made her fail
that test to begin with   she just forgot that the face of a
clock had a twelve and remembered that the current
president of the United States was Baker   she also forgot
the other questions which made her mind stumble and fail
"the only test in my whole life"   Daddy and I kept telling
her it was okay to forget   but forgetting still made her
frown and twist her wedding ring.

a lifetime of whatnots   memory pieces given by
     Daddy's mama and great aunts   lead- crystal nappies
a ruby glass vase   hand-painted floral plates   and from
her favorite aunt in Chicago   salt and pepper shakers in

cobalt blue   crystal bowls with carved animals   el greco
thin Egyptian vases   all displayed with still life perfection
     after she had moved them from one end table to
another   one room to another   mixed with tortuously
chosen vacation mementos   she could stew for hours
     in a gift shop   just making sure   it-was-the-right-
one-perfect   the murano glass   as well as the cracker
barrel mugs   one-by-one she selected   ceremoniously
handed them   to her dearest and oldest friends from
church   the neighborhood   with a "just for you" as she
     patted their hands closed   oh and the women holding
the traffic signs on the road construction site in front of
their house   leaving a trail of her stuff   so perhaps
she could find her way back home.

I hold the receiver too tightly,

"Prepare" I'd been warned
"she'll forget you too."   I knew   but . . .
what does that even mean?   it's not like practicing
tying sewing knots   by rolling the thread around my finger
*   then sliding it off   pulling it tight   so it would hold.*

"Hi, Mama" holding my breath.

Holding Daddy in my arms as he sobbed his loss
*   his head nestled in my neck when I first saw him*
after his mother died . . .

how do I practice being motherless?

"Oh, hi, Nancy"
            I release my breath.

It is enough   one more day
it is enough.   why is it so hard
to wish for so little?

Near Silence.   Near Dark

before sleep seeps
into bone marrow . . .

I thought I was home
        then I heard
near silence
        only
        dripping faucet   in the tub
        roaring furnace   from the basement.

I thought I could sleep
        then I saw
near dark
        only
        flickering bulb   in the hallway
        waning moon   from the window.

Saturday Concert

Her head demurely bowed   while seated
at a back table in Cracker Barrel
     Mama starts to hum
then raises her head . . . sings
at the top of her lungs
along with Dolly Parton.

Daddy focuses on his french fries.
She bellows
     nods to the other patrons
who turn our way   then
just away.

She shoves back her chair
     plants her feet   stands
I grab her hand.

Daddy slouches   lowers his eyes
     works on opening a stubbornly
sealed tub of Promise to smear on his biscuits.

Waitresses balance mugs of scalding coffee
on brown plastic trays   hurry past her
     keep a wary eye   become totally deaf.

Toddlers dimple   clap
Mama dampens the rising crescendo.
Daddy spreads strawberry jam over his biscuit
     closes his eyes   takes a deliberate bite.

She pauses
     curtsies
       plops down.

thunder shower

tiny twinkles of light
          wink in new sunshine
          on the phone wire.

Vespers

Beneath the bleeps
his ragged breath so soft
I bend breath-close
"Make.
Your mother.
Stop.
Driving."

His exhausted snores
smother the incessant bleeps
as I settle into a waiting chair
in a room too sterile too tucked in.

do you know, your blue jays
still scold and bicker?
your humming birds
now flirt with the sugarless feeder?
your squirrels
have abandoned
the hull-littered ground?

lilacs bloomed and browned
peonies shattered and wait
for another dead header
only the compost
goes on.

A nurse whitely glides thru the door
reads blinking numbers
scribbles on a chart
fades away.

well, yes, mama should no longer drive—
on a good day, no problem, but she can
no longer judge her days

you told her, or tried to
and what did she do?
grabbed her keys, drove but four miles
bought ugly dresses sizes too small
years too young which now testify
in her stuffed closet with dangling hang tags

you've asked . . .
perhaps . . . ordered . . .

others advised
make her stop. call the state police.
have them come to the house. take her license.

you did not . . .

yet
she could
kill.

I stand.
Stretch.
Retreat to the incandescent hall
nod to the night nurse
drive to my childhood home
for another night of scrubbing floors
removing bloated cans from the emptying pantry
trying to pay the mounting bills
sleeping sort-of
before
grey light pries open my eyes
to dress, see that Mama is dressed
drive her for an egg mcsomething
to witness her signing papers
for tomorrow's quadruple bypass
holding Daddy's hand as he sleeps.

I stand.
Stretch.
Nod to the day nurse
usher Mama to the elevators
drive us home
secure a day-sitter
return . . .

I listen.
For
   a night.
For
   a day
Into
   a night . . .

"Mama, you can no longer drive.
You must stop."

"No.   I will show you.
I will drive us to see your dad.   I will . . . "

"Mama.
This is the hardest
thing I've ever had to tell you.
But.
You.
Can't.
You just can't drive."

Eyes blue-flame
flicker
dull.

Awareness hit me

    like the knowledge I needed a clip for my bellbottoms
    as I picked gravel out of my knees and palms
    before I stepped away from crumpled handle bars

hit me hard

    like the time I fell out of the mimosa tree
    knocking too much breath out
    so I could not even cry   knocked me wiser

only without the blood.

Long tears

      streak
            the pane.

Long tears

      streaked
            the pane.

Daughterwork
      (after she is asleep)

No skirts. No dresses. No zippers.
      match favorite tops
      with new baggy sweatpants.

Put her name in her clothes.
      over and over and over
      with permanent marker
      before
      hanging both on a single hanger.

A single hanger.

Weary. Deep hollow

  . . . even breathing is work.

Weary. Soundless
cry. Silence to clot.

weary. weary
      just weary.

As I kissed her

As I kissed her forehead
        wishing her   "Sleep tight"
        her eyes pooled   her hands trembled
        some newspaper flyer.

Night by night, she had read me to sleep
        from the *Tales of a Thousand and One Nights*
        making sure that I would not ever trade
        the old lamp for a new one.

This night
        I take the sales advertisement from her hands
        place it on her bedside table
        on top of Michener's *Space*   building a tower
        of the unread   the unreadable.

My mama is leaving printed words for
        swirls and whorls
        on the wallpaper border
        edging the ceiling
        of her newly painted room.

Still, My Mama

Her hand, rice paper skin over tiny bird bones,
reaches for an incorrigible lock
loops it over my ear
gets it out of my eyes
pats my ear to hold
—I was never sure and now it's too late to ask—
to hold back my hair or to keep my ear on?

Words

icicle

from a broken gutter.

Paring

A forward slash
halfway across my middle finger's tip
right above the first joint
long clotted, scabbed, healed, faded.

"Watch what you are doing.
Be careful with that knife . . . "

Mama hadn't finished
when the paring knife hit the apple seed
and pretty-as-you-please
laid open my finger to the bone.

"Here. Hold this napkin tight against your finger."

"No. I'm not taking her for stitches.
This little scar will remind her of her folly."

I bit my tongue until it bled
and tasted my blood's salt.

As I massage lotion into her hands . . . I wait
for her to voice her pleasure   to ignite . . .
while I try to rub smooth, hard, white lines
from both our hands.

February

sounds as white
      as the snow,

covering all
      with flows
      of nothing
      and nothingness.

Rituals

"I bought her a rosebud and vase" my father said "had to go
to two places to find one   people just don't seem to buy
them much anymore   had to put the vase at the Nurse's
Station   they said last year   one of the patients went in
your mother's room   ate the petals."

surely not rose hip tea   but maybe like crystallized violets?
a bit of happy . . . so like carnival cotton candy
    I hope Mama ate them.

"That is so like you   what a thoughtful gesture."
He guides the conversation to a recent funeral he attended

    winded   exhausted from finals   study marathons   I arrived
from college with only minutes to spare at church . . . my suitcases—
full of laundry—were in the foyer where my ride home had dumped them
to the smiles of the ushers   the candles already lit   flickered in the
windows   the introit laced through the parishioners

in the choir room   Daddy held a robe nearly my size for me to slip over
my jeans and sweat shirt   handed me a music folder with a bulletin
and the night's music . . . the choir director slipped a white stole
over my head   tried to smooth my hair in place   pointed to where I
belonged in the processional . . . so began Christmas Eve's midnight
service   I had given up the battle of saying I didn't want to sing
hadn't practiced   didn't know where to sit   was just plain tired from
finals   the choir director knew I'd sing   none of us could disagree
with the choir's only bass   when he cared so much   for us just to sing
    all together

"Who all was there?"   he began listing the mourners
how they were related   the pall bearers

    once I'd marched   sang   finally settled in the uncomfortable
wooden pew   while the Christ Candle was being lit   I could study

the faces of the worshippers   see who was there and with whom
*   when I spied a woman I knew only by her first name*
because we shared first names

she worked down town in a dress shop   it sold seconds   I had been
buying dresses there since early high school   she'd on occasion tuck
one back   one that she thought I might really like   one which didn't
have too much mending to do   to make it presentable   an occasional
sweater dress or an oversized sweater   to go with my college uniform of
jeans   while I tried on the clothes   in the community dressing room
*   she'd ask about college   my boyfriend   our dates   she might*
even ask how classes were going

she was just beautiful   violet eyes   black hair   glossy lips
*   and for the longest time   I'd thought she had so many boyfriends*
older than she was   but well-dressed   I'd see her holding a man's
arm   as they walked down Broadway   going to lunch or dinner
*   eventually   even I figured out   that nobody had that many*
boyfriends   but by then   I considered her a friend   I just didn't tell
Mama my conclusion

"Did the choir sing?"   his voice picked up tempo as he
continued to answer

there she was near the back of the church   dressed in red velvet
with sprigs of green holly in her hair   with perhaps six or eight
other women I didn't know   they were all smiling   singing hymns
*   she was sitting next to one older woman   probably Mama's age*

when the service ended   after we'd sung all of the verses to the
recessional hymn   Silent Night   had all blown out our candles
*   before I even returned the choir robe   looked for my luggage in the*
coat room where somebody always stowed it . . . I went to find her   all
the church bells were announcing   "Christmas had come!"

"Nancy! Welcome! Merry Christmas!" in spite of Miss Elizabeth's
frumpy frown my way—the same one she had given me all my life to
hush my giggle fits—I gave Nancy a big holiday hug "So glad you could
be here tonight . . ." as she hugged me back   she whispered in my ear
    "Remember this   not for now   but for someday   your father
was always   always"—she drew out that word to   its full length—
"a gentleman   to everyone"   she turned quickly   followed her
friends out into the night.

Now   now is that someday.

He was   is   to her   to them   in every bar in three
counties where he sold whiskey   bantering with the bar
owners   the bar tenders   cleaning crews   all the working
people   now   to the nurses   social workers   cleaning
crews   all the patients   their families   to Mama   an-
offer-his-arm   hold-a-door-open   pick-up-a-dropped
scarf   nod-and-speak gentleman.

"Your mother was so pleased that I brought her a rose   she
kept telling me   but I had to leave   she told me 'I just love
real flowers' about twenty times   and I did have to go to the
funeral . . ."

"I know Daddy. I know   "I'm glad you found the rose for
Mama."

"Me too" he says just a little too quietly
before I hear the click.

Thief
of all you have stolen

I am most angry
that you pilfered my name.

"Doll?" she smiles up at my face
asking the same of nurses and orderlies.

I pat her hand and smile
"I'm here, Mama."

Replicating itself

"one-more-time"
breath whispers

you don't understand, Mama
when I tell you that your granddaughter
is carrying your next great grandchild
your mind has forgotten how to spark

A Day Flower

Mama's taken to her bed
refusing to walk
even down the hall
and back, a day lily
closing in on herself.

In my dreams
the touch of her hand on
my nightmare forehead
tells me
I will be alright.

Another August Anniversary

"Your dad just said he loved me" Mama stage-whispers.

She always begins this story with "When he got a leave
        I met him at the train station.   With the preacher."

Brittle sepia . . .
a svelte bride in satin   hair I knew had been bronze
same color   she always said   as my daughter's
cascaded in barely controlled curls
*   styled in Kentucky humidity*
a solemn groom tall in his Army uniform   eyes dark
scorched serious   memory scars   European Theater of
Operations Ribbon   studded with five Bronze Stars
*   pinned to his chest.*

Bud, Daddy's best man, presented the newlyweds
enough gasoline rations from his farming allotment
to get them to St. Louis and back—knowing he'd have to
plow the river bottoms with the mule—their honeymoon
a weekend   a tour through a beer brewery   through an
unairconditioned brewery   then to Daddy's parents' house
    the rest of his two-week leave . . . shared with his brother
a new sister-in-law . . .

Just last month   Daddy made clear   "When you've been
married   as long as we have   you become a part of
each other.   I'm a part of her   she's a part of me.   This
will be the first time   in sixty-two years   we've been
apart on our anniversary."

A part and apart.

Mama's voice silkens   "It'll be okay" she coos.

"It'll be okay."

So unlike the days of before   she doesn't have words
    of how to continue now   so in a blink   "Here
talk to your daughter."

"Is it hot there? Here the grass crunches under my sandals.
Too dry. Too dry." Minuets of   words and silences
    choreographed through months of practice   I fill up
white spaces   "Too hot here   the window units only hold
at seventy-eight   better than the one-o-one outside."

I tell my childish self   *keep talking*
"I bought Mama a Hershey bar
said it was from you."

He dry sobs.

"Mama's eating it now.   Does she ever love her chocolate.
Had to keep it in the freezer overnight
    it's starting to melt now, but she is smiling at me."

"From your Dad" she whispers   smiles
with her teeth   lips   chin smeared with chocolate.

Shift   please   help me   shift
"Have you had your lunch? What did you have?"

He slides   nearly falls   rights himself   finds solid
ground
"Turkey bacon and tomato sandwich."

I could honestly laugh   "Are you still frying up
a whole pound   freezing it   taking out a few slices
each day?"

"Yep. Saves me time that way. Oh and dishes."
    His turn to lead   his voice loosens   in the long-legged

loping of the salesman   "I'm stayin' inside   watchin'
television   eatin' a lot   I mean   a lot   of ice cream."

We are okay now.
"Gotta go   there is melting chocolate everywhere.
Even on her elbow."

"Tell her . . .
just tell her . . ."

"I will . . .
We love you too   'bye."

"Mama, Daddy said to tell you   to tell you   "
she just smiles   *perhaps forgetting this is her anniversary*
their anniversary   forgetting hertheir wedding   hertheir youth
    hertheir . . .

I grab what is left of a paper napkin on the unwashed table in
this room   this community room of others—all rocking
swaying   repeating over and over single words   repeating
sounds—I cannot say what I will   what I must
just not yet   not this second   "Here   let me wipe this
chocolate off your face."

    I dig in my jeans' pocket   find a remnant of a tissue
spit on it   begin to rub clean her face—a face
so like her oldest grandson's face   on his second
birthday   eating his birthday cake
chocolate, of course.

This   this   I know how to fix.

So I shed these

      and even though
      I know I will not need them

I glance back   just once
      and see them torn and tattered
      in the nodding dusk.

Time Markers

Mama blew
            the whole fuse box
            burned out the wiring
            as she cooked her French
            Provincial clay clocks
            in the basement.

Daddy whistled
            while he rewired the basement
            removed singed boards and smells
            so her kiln could crackle
            special glazes on pastel petals
            without burning us down.

Mama changed
            from frying to broiling
            about their twentieth year
            after Daddy's ulcer healed
            enough for him to grumble
            over his new diet.

Daddy splurged
            on a new periwinkle blue sports car
            for Mama with their first
            unneeded money
            said her eyes picked up the color
            of its newly hand-waxed surface.

Mama and Daddy held hands
            in church after he had escorted
            her from her nursing home so
            she'd still be able
            to see the stained glass windows
            and other best friends.

Daddy stopped eating
    just gave up
    six days before their anniversary—
    the first
    he would've celebrated
    alone.

Equinox

tremble to flame
flicker by breeze
smother in moth dust

until
moth and soot
merge.

Remembrances

Dried-blood roses
        brittle.

Dried blood
        roses brittle.

for tomorrows.

Raking
        from the fallen rock wall
        decaying piles of clutter

restacking
        on the solid stone base
        tumbling yesterdays . . .

Nancy Genevieve with her mother in the Alzheimer's Unit
six days before her mother's passing

Nancy was a storyteller before she could read. She was a writer before she could write. She copied the words she saw in her mother's Gregg shorthand book and then read her writings to her parents. Kentucky's heritage—Nancy and her family's five-generation heritage—percolated through the same limestone which gives the state's bourbon it distinctive flavor and its thoroughbreds their competitive strength and Nancy's work its images and attitude.

For over thirty years in Kentucky and Illinois, Nancy has celebrated with her high school and college students the joy and power of writing, served as a fiction editor and a special online editor for two, international journals, and edited eleven volumes of her students' creative non-fiction.

Nancy's poetry, fiction, and creative non-fiction pieces have appeared in numerous literary journals. *NYX: Sister of Erebus A Memoir of My Mother's Alzheimer's* is the final volume of the NYX trilogy; *NYX: Mother of Light* was published in 2001 and *NYX: Daughter of Chaos* in 2002. She and her husband live in New England.